GLORIOUS CATS

GLORIOUS CATS

THE PAINTINGS OF
LESLEY ANNE IVORY

CRESCENT BOOKS
NEW YORK ● AVENEL

With love to Linda

Introduction copyright © 1989 by Lesley Anne Ivory
Illustrations copyright © 1989 by Lesley Anne Ivory
Text selection and design copyright © 1989, 1991 by
Russell Ash & Bernard Higton

Conceived, edited and designed by
Russell Ash and Bernard Higton

This 1995 edition published by Crescent Books,
distributed by Random House Value Publishing, Inc.
40 Engelhard Avenue, Avenel, New Jersey 07001.

Random House
New York ● Toronto ● London ● Sydney ● Auckland

A CIP catalog record for this book is available from the Library of Congress.

ISBN 0-517-14227-9

10,9,8,7,6,5,4,3,2,1

Manufactured in China

Introduction

'Why do you paint cats?' I am frequently asked. I paint cats because I love them. I love their grace and beauty. I feel perfectly in tune with them and, as an artist, their every movement is a challenge and source of inspiration to me. Cats are glorious creatures — who must on no account be underestimated. They are clean, intelligent, friendly and caring. Their eyes are fathomless depths of cat-world mysteries.

'And the rich backgrounds?' When I was a child my mother, who was a textile designer, used to let me look through her albums of fabric designs, her watercolours of flowers and her collection of post-cards of works of art, and I would pore over each one, delighting in the intricacies of ancient tapestries, and Botticelli paintings. Eventually, my twin loves of cats and finely detailed backgrounds came together when I was struck with the idea of painting a Persian cat on a Persian carpet, and from this has grown my preoccupation with portraying cats in a multitude of appropriate settings.

I love bringing the cats and their backgrounds together, and in my work I try to evoke the individual character and aura of every cat. Each painting takes many hours of total concentration to achieve the desired result as I strive to depict every hair and every whisker with complete faithfulness to my sitter. I hope that you will enjoy the fruits of my labours as much as I have enjoyed painting them for you.

Lesley Anne Ivory

To a Cat

Nelly, methinks, 'twixt thee and me
    There is a kind of sympathy;
And could we interchange our nature, –
If I were cat, thou human creature, –
I should, like thee, be no great mouser,
And thou, like me, no great composer;
For, like thy plaintive mews, my muse
With villainous whine doth date abuse,
Because it hath not made me sleek
As golden down on Cupid's cheek;
And yet thou canst upon the rug lie,
Stretch'd out like snail, or curl'd up snugly,
As if thou wert not lean or ugly;
And I, who in poetic flights
Sometimes complain of sleepless nights,
Am apt to doze till past eleven, –
The world would just the same go round
If I were hang'd and thou wert drown'd;
There is one difference, 'tis true, –
Thou dost not know it, and I do.

HARTLEY COLERIDGE

The Mystical Cat

No other animal has managed to get itself tangled up in as much legend, myth, symbolism, religion, history and human affairs as the cat. From the time it first appeared upon the scene some four thousand years ago, it has played its part in almost every age. And indeed, one of the chief and yet unsolved mysteries connected with this animal is that before the earliest Egyptian dynasties and wall decorations, there is no record of this animal at all, neither in cave art or kitchen middens. It is as though it suddenly appeared on earth, neatly packaged and with all its qualities, practically as we know it today.

Are we, as its devotees, hoping that some of this marvel and mystery will rub off on us by cultivating it and thus elevate us a cut above the rest of the herd?

Black magic, white magic, good luck and bad, a hundred superstitions covering every aspect of human life and condition, are ascribed to the cat. It became the familiar of witches, the companion of the devil and, of course, a god in its own right.

PAUL GALLICO

The Fur Coat

I walked out in my Coat of Pride;
I looked about on every side;

And said the mountains should not be
Just where they were, and that the sea

Was out of place, and that the beech
Should be an oak! and then, from each,

I turned in dignity, as if
They were not there! I sniffed a sniff;

And climbed upon my sunny shelf;
And sneezed a while; and scratched myself.

JAMES STEPHENS

Mademoiselle

This animal was affectionate and winning, but maniacal and wily. She would not permit any vagaries, any deviation, she intended that one should go to bed and get up at the same time. When she was discontented, she expressed in the darkness of her look nuances of irritation that her master never mistook. If he returned before eleven o'clock at night, she was waiting for him at the door, in the entrance-hall, scratching the wood, meowing before he had entered the room. Then she would roll her languorous pupils of greeny gold, rub herself against his breeches, jump on the furniture, stand herself upright to look like a small horse rearing, and when he came near her, still arching her back give him, in friendship, great blows with her head. If it were after eleven o'clock she did not go up to him, but restricted herself to getting up only when he came near her, still arching her back but not caressing him. If it were later still, she would not move and she would complain grumblingly.

J.-K. HUYSMANS

Mother Cat

Leaving the greying dawn, to rest,
The huntress returns to her nest
Of kittens, a plump little heap
Where they lie curled up in restless sleep.
She wakes them with low singing cries,
Then stretched out she lies
To still the hunger of her pushing young.
Lovingly with her raspberry tongue
She keeps each round wriggling shape
(though protesting) immaculate.
Then satisfied, they sleep with pearl-like toes
Clustered around each little pink nose.
She listens to their contented sighs,
Her pride, like fire in her shining eyes.

BARBARA ESKIL

Chinese Cat

How many ages
Of Chinese ancestry
In the fine pages
Of your sleek history
Must there be, feline,
Tortuous mystery?
Skeins of the night that
Silkened the sky
Over dusty pagodas
Glimmering lie
Down your long sides;
And, thinner than water,
Like water glides
Your bland shadow
Along the floor.
How many cinnamon
Blossoms bore
Delicate shade through
Nightingaled hours,
In that remoter
Life that was yours
Down by the yellow,
Asian sea,

In lustrous mellow
Antiquity?
In towers of jade
And minarets ashen
With dawn, did an idol
Dream and fashion
Your slithe and beautiful
Demoniacal
Movement of fur,
And the curded sound
Of your inward purr?
Where did he find
The gloomy, sunny
Spheres of your eyes
Like globules of honey?
Under the velvet
Fall of your paws
Needles the light of your
Polished claws . . .
Were you a Favorite
Ages ago,
Who purred at an Emperor's
Overthrow?

MARTHA OSTENSO

The Golden Cat

Great is the Golden Cat who treads
    The Blue Roof Garden o'er our heads,
The never tired smiling One
That Human People call the Sun.

He stretches forth his paw at dawn
And though the blinds are closely drawn
His claws peep through like Rays of Light,
To catch the fluttering Bird of Night.

He smiles into the Hayloft dim
And the brown Hay smiles back at him,
And when he strokes the Earth's green fur
He makes the Fields and Meadows purr.

His face is one big Golden smile,
It measures round, at least a mile –
How dull our World would be, and flat,
Without the Golden Pussy Cat!

OLIVER HERFORD

The Elegant Cat

Seraphita was of a dreamy and contemplative disposition. She would sit on a cushion for hours together, quite motionless, not asleep, and following with her eyes, in a rapture of attention, sights invisible to mere mortals. Caresses were agreeable to her, but she returned them in a very reserved manner and only in the case of persons whom she favoured with her rarely-accorded esteem. She was fond of luxury, and it was always upon the handsomest easy chair, or the rug that would best show off her snowy fur, that she would surely be found. She devoted a great deal of her time to her toilet; her glossy coat was carefully smoothed every morning. She washed herself with her paw, and licked every atom of her fur with her pink tongue until it shone like new silver. When anyone touched her she instantly effaced all trace of the contact; she could not endure to be tumbled. An idea of aristocracy was suggested by her elegance and distinction, and among her own people she was a duchess at least. She delighted in perfumes, would stick her nose into bouquets, bite scented handkerchiefs with little spasms of pleasure, and walk about among the scent-bottles on the toilet-table, smelling at their stoppers; no doubt she would have used the powder-puff if she had been permitted. Such was Seraphita, and never did cat more amply justify a poetic name . . .

THEOPHILE GAUTIER

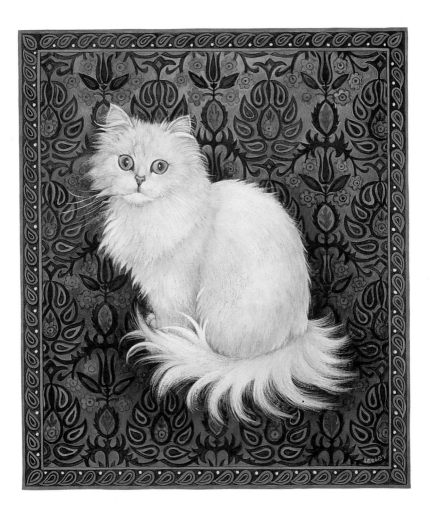

'In Honour of Taffy Topaz'

Taffy, the topaz-coloured cat,
Thinks now of this and now of that,
But chiefly of his meals,
Asparagus, and cream, and fish,
Are objects of his Freudian wish;
What you don't give, he steals.

His gallant heart is strongly stirred
By chink of plate or flight of bird,
He has a plumy tail;
At night he treads on stealthy pad
As merry as Sir Galahad
A-seeking of the Grail.

His amiable amber eyes
Are very friendly, very wise;
Like Buddha, grave and fat,
He sits, regardless of applause,
And thinking, as he kneads his paws,
What fun to be a cat!

CHRISTOPHER MORLEY

The Cosmic Cat

My cat is winningly indifferent.
Exquisitely present, perfectly apart.
She accepts a caress with sensuous completeness
Yet she is company and no boon companion.
She sits in my soft armchair,
Her eyes half-closed, her face a secret place
Where whiskers move. She does not disturb
By a possessive eye, uncritical with love,
But broods with an omniscient inattention,
Like the curved sky,
So far above the teeming only earth
Where masters slave protesting all their lives,
And cats hold court in idleness,
And none survives save the written cat
And the remembered man.

JOHN INGLIS HALL

The Night Cat

I am not alone in the room;
   A bright intelligence
Watches the fire in the gloom
   Of Winter's imminence;

Watches, and waits for the hour
   When something worthy to do
Shall make its every power
   Alert, vivid and new;

When out of a darker lair
   In the hidden haunts of the house
There shall glide into the open air
   For a single moment a mouse;

When the still chirp of a bird,
   In ears that are veiled in fur,
Even in sleep is heard,
   As the lithe muscles stir.

It knows the way of the night,
   What wanders and at what hours:
Scents tell it, and sight,
   And a knowledge older than ours.

When the day is gone with his wrath,
   And the night is hushed, it will roam.
As the needle points to the North,
   So it turns towards home.

Wisdom it has from of yore
   Touching all things that concern it,
And all that I know of its lore
   Is that I shall never learn it.

LORD DUNSANY

LESLEY

The Cat of the House

Over the hearth with my 'minishing eyes I muse
        Until after
The last coal dies.
Every tunnel of the mouse,
Every channel of the cricket,
I have smelt.
I have felt
The secret shifting of the mouldered rafter,
And heard
Every bird in the thicket.
I see
You
Nightingale up in your tree!
I, born of a race of strange things,
Of deserts, great temples, great kings,
In the hot sands where the nightingale never sings!

FORD MADOX FORD

Cats Observed

She is a sprightly cat, hardly past her youth; so, happening to move the fringe of the rug a little with our foot, she darts out a paw, and begins plucking it and inquiring into the matter, as if it were a challenge to play, or something lively enough to be eaten. What a graceful action of that foot of hers, between delicacy and petulance! – combining something of a thrust out, a beat, and a scratch. There seems even something of a little bit of fear in it, as if just enough to provoke her courage, and give her the excitement of a sense of hazard. We remember being much amused with seeing a kitten manifestly making a series of experiments upon the patience of its mother, trying how far the latter would put up with positive bites and thumps. The kitten ran at her every moment, gave her a knock or a bite of the tail; and then ran back again, to recommence the assault. The mother sat looking at her, as if betwixt tolerance and admiration, to see how far the spirit of the family was inherited or improved by her sprightly offspring. At length, however, the 'little Pickle' presumed too far, and the mother, lifting up her paw, and meeting her at the very nick of the moment, gave her one of the most unsophisticated boxes of the ear we ever beheld. It sent her rolling half over the room, and made her come to a most ludicrous pause, with the oddest little look of premature and wincing meditation.

LEIGH HUNT

Cat on the Mat

The fat cat on the mat
   may seem to dream
of nice mice that suffice
   for him, or cream;
but he is free, maybe,
   walks in thought
unbowed, proud, where loud
   roared and fought
his kin, lean and slim,
   or deep in den
in the East feasted on beasts
   and tender men.

The giant lion with iron
   claw in paw,
and huge ruthless tooth
   in gory jaw;
the pard dark-starred
   fleet upon feet,
that oft soft from aloft
   leaps on his meet
where words loom in gloom —
   far now they be
   fierce and free,
   and tamed is he;
but fat cat on the mat
kept as pet
he does not forget.

J. R. R. TOLKIEN

The Musical Cat

You could never accuse him of idleness, and yet he knew the secret of repose. The poet who wrote so prettily of him that his little life was rounded with a sleep understated his facility: it was rounded with a good many. His conscience never seemed to interfere with his slumbers. In fact, he had good habits and a contented mind. I can see him now walk in at the study door, sit down by my chair, bring his tail artistically about his feet, and look up at me with unspeakable happiness in his handsome face. I often thought that he felt the dumb limitation which denied him the power of language. But since he was denied speech, he scorned the inarticulate mouthings of the lower animals. The vulgar mewing and yowling of the cat species was beneath him; he sometimes uttered a sort of well-bred and articulate ejaculation, when he wished to call attention to something that he considered remarkable, or to some want of his, but he never went whining about. He could sit for hours at a closed window, when he desired to enter, without a murmur, and when it was opened he never admitted that he had been impatient by 'bolting' in. Though speech he had not, and the unpleasant kind of utterance given to his race he would not use, he had a mighty power of purr to express his measureless content with congenial society. There was in him a musical organ with stops of varied power and expression, upon which I have no doubt he could have performed Scarlatti's celebrated cat-fugue.

CHARLES DUDLEY WARNER

A Cat's Example

For three whole days I and my cat
    Have come up here, and patiently sat –
    We sit and wait on silent Time;
He for a mouse that scratched close by,
At a hole where he sets his eye –
    And I for some music and rhyme.

Is this the Poet's secret, that
He waits in patience, like this cat,
    To start a dream from under cover?
A cat's example, too, in love,
With Passion's every trick and move,
    Would burn up any human lover.

W. H. DAVIES

——— A Favourite Cat ———

I took my beautiful puss today
  (Sleek and fluffy and bland was she),
And set her down on the hearth to play
  (Beloved as only a cat may be).

My hand would tickle her velvet paws
  (Black and velvety paws had she)
And toy with the innocent-seeming claws,
  Sheathed as only a cat's may be.

Soft and deep was her coat so bright
  (Deep and soft, like a starless sea);
And her eyes were lit with a far, strange light —
  Mystic, subtle, with love for me.

So I fell to wondering (as she lay
  Close to the fire as a cat may be)
If, centuries since, we twain were one,
  Lit with the hopes of the days to be.

Perhaps: who knows? Yet if such be true
  (Whisper the secret, Fluff, to me!)
Much would it help me to comprehend
  That haunting flame in the eyes of thee.

Perchance, by shores of some deep lagoon,
  Thy face met mine — as it now meets me;
By Nilus' banks, 'neath an Afric moon,
  I told my love — as I now tell thee.

EDWARD HENRY BLAKENEY

This is My Chair

This is my chair.
  Go away and sit somewhere else.
This one is all my own.
It is the only thing in your house that I possess
And insist upon possessing.
Everything else therein is yours.
My dish,
My toys,
My basket,
My scratching post and my Ping-Pong ball;
You provided them for me.
This chair I selected for myself.
I like it,
It suits me.
You have the sofa,
The stuffed chair
And the footstool.
I don't go and sit on them do I?
Then why cannot you leave me mine,
And let us have no further argument?

PAUL GALLICO

Cats in Ancient Egypt

A very great number of Cats' mummies, discovered in Egypt, afford ample proof of the esteem in which Pussy was held in Thebes' streets three thousand years ago. If one died a natural death, it was mourned for with many ceremonies; among others the entire household, where the death took place, shaved off their eyebrows. If killed, the murderer was given up to the mob to buffet him to death. Cats were held sacred when alive, and when they died were embalmed and deposited in the niches of the catacombs. An insult offered by a Roman to a Cat once caused an insurrection among the Egyptians when nothing else would excite them. Cambyses gained Pelusis, which had previously successfully resisted all attacks, by the following stratagem: he gave to each of his soldiers employed in the attack a live Cat, instead of a buckler, and the Egyptians, rather than hurt the objects of their veneration, suffered themselves to be vanquished without striking a blow.

C. H. ROSS

Under-the-table manners

I t's very hard to be polite
  If you're a cat.
When other folks are up at table
Eating all that they are able,
   You are down upon the mat
   If you're a cat

You're expected just to sit
   If you're a cat.
Not to let them know you're there
By scratching on the chair,
   Or a light, respected pat
   If you're a cat

You are not to make a fuss
   If you're a cat
Tho' there's fish upon the plate
You're expected just to wait,
   Wait politely on the mat
   If you're a cat.

ANON

On a Night of Snow

Cat, if you go outdoors you must walk in the snow.
   You will come back with little white shoes on your feet,
Little white slippers of snow that have heels of sleet.
Stay by the fire, my Cat. Lie still, do not go.
See how the flames are leaping and hissing low,
I will bring you a saucer of milk like a marguerite,
So white and so smooth, so spherical and so sweet —
Stay with me, Cat. Outdoors the wild winds blow.

Outdoors the wild winds blow, Mistress, and dark is the night.
Strange voices cry in the trees, intoning strange lore;
And more than cats move, lit by our eyes' green light,
On silent feet where the meadow grasses hang hoar —
Mistress, there are portents abroad of magic and might,
And things that are yet to be done. Open the door!

ELIZABETH COATSWORTH

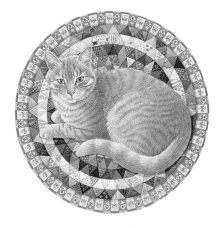